The Question & Answer Book

ALL ABOUT DESERTS

ALL ABOUT DESERTS

By John Sanders
Illustrated by Patti Boyd

Troll Associates

Library of Congress Cataloging in Publication Data

Sanders, John (John Michael)
    All about deserts.

    (Question and answer book)
    Summary: Uses a question and answer format to present
basic information about deserts, such as how they were
formed, how plants and animals live, and the usefulness
of deserts.
    1. Deserts—Juvenile literature. [1. Deserts.
2. Questions and answers] I. Boyd, Patti, ill.
II. Title. III. Series.
GB611.S26   1984   508.315´4   83-4857
ISBN 0-89375-965-1
ISBN 0-89375-966-X (pbk.)

Printed in the United States of America
10   9   8   7   6   5   4   3

What is a desert?

A desert is a land that is like no other on this amazing earth of ours.

It doesn't have the leafy greenery of other lands. It is harsh and forbidding, with great extremes of climate—from burning heat to freezing cold. The strange land of the desert almost seems to dare anything to survive on it.

Scientists who study the earth say deserts are parched, dry lands, where rain almost never falls.

What are "dry" deserts?

Dry deserts are lands that get less than 10 inches (25 centimeters) of rain a year. The world's largest hot, dry desert is the Sahara in North Africa, where daytime temperatures regularly reach 120 degrees Fahrenheit (49 degrees Celsius) or more. Other dry deserts are found in the southwestern part of the United States, Arabia, Australia, and South America.

What are "cold" deserts?

Most people think of very high temperatures and dry, sandy land when they think of deserts, but some of the world's deserts do not fit that description. These other deserts are the *cold* deserts.

The polar regions of the Arctic and Antarctic are cold deserts. In these regions, temperatures are so low that very little frozen snow and ice melt, and little rain falls. These conditions make it hard for plants, animals, and people to survive.

How much of the world is desert?

Deserts cover about one-fifth of the earth! If you could see them from high above, the world's hot, dry deserts would look like two belts stretching all the way around the earth. These two belts fall above and below the *equator*, the imaginary line that divides the earth in half.

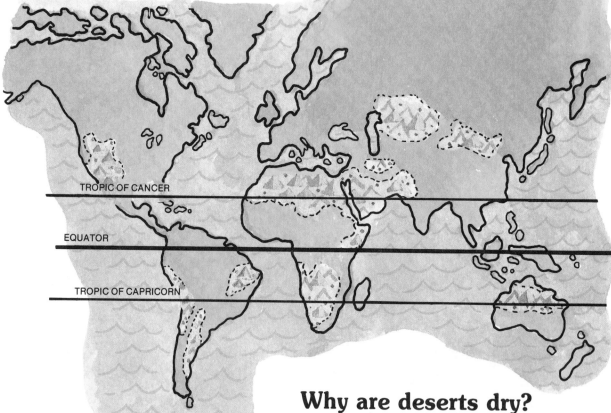

TROPIC OF CANCER

EQUATOR

TROPIC OF CAPRICORN

Why are deserts dry?

Before you can understand why the deserts of the world are dry, you first must know how they were formed. Let's step back in time to see what happened to turn so much of the earth into desert land.

How were deserts formed?

Ever since life began, the earth has been wrapped in a blanket of air called the *atmosphere*.

The winds of the atmosphere constantly swirled around the earth in swiftly moving air currents. As they dipped over the ocean, the air currents picked up moisture. As they traveled over the land, they dropped their moisture as rain or snow.

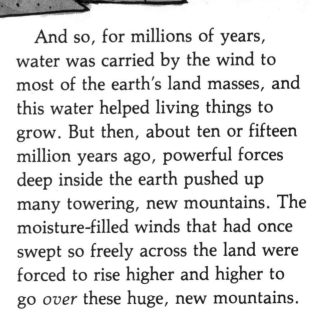

And so, for millions of years, water was carried by the wind to most of the earth's land masses, and this water helped living things to grow. But then, about ten or fifteen million years ago, powerful forces deep inside the earth pushed up many towering, new mountains. The moisture-filled winds that had once swept so freely across the land were forced to rise higher and higher to go *over* these huge, new mountains.

9

As the winds rose higher in the sky, they cooled, causing the moisture they carried to turn into rain or snow. But the rain and snow fell mostly on the side of the mountains facing the *ocean*. There was little moisture left to fall on the *other* side of the mountain.

Now there were no moisture-carrying clouds to provide shade. In the hot sun, the land on the far side of these new mountain ranges grew drier. The winds still blew, but now they were hot, dry winds, and they dried out the land even more.

High barrier mountains robbed the land of its normal rainfall. Hot sun and hot winds dried out the land. These were the main natural causes of the deserts—the so-called *deserted lands*. And to this day, these are two reasons why the deserts are so dry.

How are deserts alike?

No two deserts—or even parts of the same desert—are exactly alike. Yet all of them, except for the icy polar deserts, have much in common.

They look alike. They are bare, eaten away, eroded. They have steep mountains, high flat lands called *plateaus*, deep valleys, and broad flatlands.

They feel alike. They are hot during the day because there are few trees or shrubs to block the rays of the sun. And they are cold at night because there are no clouds to keep the heat from rising once the sun goes down.

All deserts are alike in another way. Each desert has its own very special sort of plants and animals. These living things are special because each has managed to *adapt*, or change, to survive in the harsh, dry world of the desert.

11

Can you imagine?

Imagine you are walking through the desert. The sun is hot. The air is dry and heavy. In the distance, beautiful colors—purples, tans, and silvery grays—shimmer in the heat of the desert sun. The air is so clear that you can see for miles. It seems as if you could almost touch the mountains towering in the distance.

Next, you "hear" the desert stillness. It is a silence so deep that it seems as if time has somehow stopped. You seem to be all alone in a strange world.

But you are *not* alone.

In the bright desert light, a huge-eared jack rabbit suddenly bounds away in high, soaring leaps. With a sharp clicking sound, a Gila woodpecker busily chips away at a giant cactus. The woodpecker is searching for insects to eat.

There are plants and shrubs and oddly shaped trees growing among the rocks and in the desert sand. Each one grows far apart from the others, so its roots have enough room to search for precious, life-giving water.

A chuckwalla lizard nibbles at the flowers of a low-growing cactus. And nearby is a horned lizard. It uncovers an anthill and begins feasting on the ants.

The tracks of a bull snake stretch across the sand until they disappear under a rock. On top of the rock, a desert tortoise suns itself.

Here and there, a furry head pokes up from an underground burrow. Or a pair of beady eyes peers around a tree trunk.

Life is all around you.

What plants live in the desert?

What lives—and thrives—in the desert? The list begins with an amazing number of plants—trees, shrubs, grasses, weeds, even flowers.

Desert plants are quite different from plants that grow in moister lands. They *must* be if they are to live with little water and in extreme temperatures.

Desert plants must find and store precious water whenever it is available. They must rest, lying *dormant*, when there is no water. And they must protect their scarce water supply from other plants and animals.

How do desert plants survive?

The ways in which desert plants have adapted are often strange and sometimes amazing.

Some plants are "water seekers." They may send their roots down as far as 100 feet (30 meters) below the ground. There, they find underground streams or other deeply buried water. Or they may have roots that spread out in all directions searching for water.

CACTUS WITH LITTLE WATER

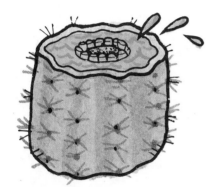

CACTUS FULL OF WATER

Other plants are "water storers." Almost everything about the cactus plant is designed to help it store water. Its wide, shallow root system can take in a huge amount of water very quickly. Its fleshy stem is able to hold all the water the roots drink in. The stem can even expand like an accordion to make room for more water. Then as the water is used up, the cactus stem folds in once more and waits for the next rain.

How do desert plants keep their water?

When desert plants get the water they need, they try to keep from losing it too quickly. Plants lose water through their leaves. This is called *transpiration*. So some desert plants have very tiny leaves. Some have "waterproof" leaves that have waxy coverings to protect them. Many plants have sharp thorns or spines to keep thirsty animals away. And one—the amazing creosote bush—actually gives off a chemical that poisons any other plant growing too close to its water-gathering territory.

What is a "drought evader"?

Besides plants that are water seekers and water storers, some desert plants are drought evaders. This means that they die during the long dry spells. But before they die, they leave seeds to start new plants. When, at last, it rains again, the seeds come to life. In just a few short weeks, these new plants are able to grow as much as many other plants would grow in a year. The seeds sprout quickly. They grow rapidly and burst into beautiful flowers. Suddenly, the sandy desert becomes a dazzling garden of colorful blooms. Then, once these plants flower, they die, leaving a new crop of seeds on the ground, waiting for the next rain.

What animals live in the desert?

Animals of all kinds have found special ways to survive in the desert. Most of the small desert mammals are burrowers. They include mice, rats, ground squirrels, rabbits, kit foxes, and badgers. They sleep all day in cool underground holes and come out at night to search for food and water.

The reptiles of the desert include lizards, tortoises, and snakes. They are cold-blooded, which means their bodies stay about the same temperature as their surroundings. So the reptiles move from sun to shade to keep from getting too hot or too cold. They often lie in the sun, soaking up its heat. But when it gets too hot, they crawl under a rock to cool off.

When a violent rainstorm takes place in the dry desert, one of nature's most amazing miracles takes place. This is the almost instant hatching of thousands of tiny shrimp eggs in the puddles left by the rain.

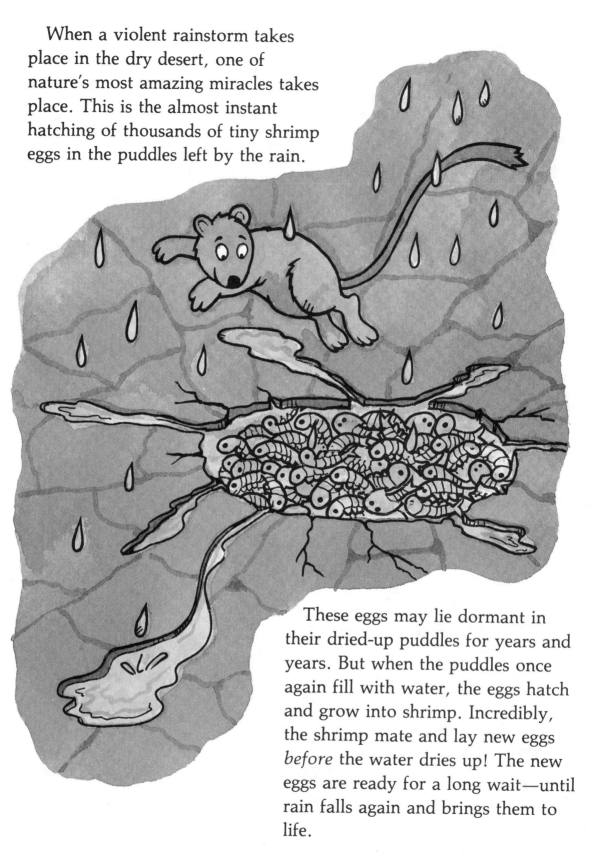

These eggs may lie dormant in their dried-up puddles for years and years. But when the puddles once again fill with water, the eggs hatch and grow into shrimp. Incredibly, the shrimp mate and lay new eggs *before* the water dries up! The new eggs are ready for a long wait—until rain falls again and brings them to life.

Which animal is the "ship of the desert"?

The camel is sometimes called the "ship of the desert." This is because it has long transported people and goods across the deserts of Asia and Africa.

The camel is perhaps the best-known and best-adapted animal of the desert. To help it walk upon the sand, the camel has broad pads on its feet. In a sandstorm, its nostrils and eyelids are able to shut tightly to keep out blowing sand. And this animal's tongue and lips are so tough, it can eat plants that have sharp or thorny leaves.

Most amazing of all, the camel can go without food and water for days, living off the fat in the hump on its back.

How do desert animals get the water they need?

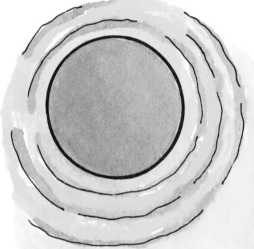

Each desert animal, no matter how big or small, needs food and water to survive. And each has adapted in its own special way to fill that need.

The tiny kangaroo rat lives on a diet of dry seeds. It almost never drinks water. Yet, this amazing creature actually produces the water it needs from the dry seeds.

The desert tortoise, on the other hand, carries along its own water supply in two water sacs inside its body.

Most desert meat-eaters, such as badgers and bobcats, are skilled hunters. They hunt at night because most of the creatures that they eat only come out then.

In the desert, nearly every living thing is a source of food and water for another, *larger* living thing. The plants gather and store water. Tiny animals eat the water-filled plants or their seeds. Larger animals eat the smaller ones. Still larger animals, in turn, eat *them*. At the very top of that food chain is one more creature —the human.

What people live in the desert?

For as far back as history can be traced, people have lived in the desert. But unlike plants and animals, they have never been able to adapt physically to desert surroundings.

Groups of wanderers, called *nomads*, cross the desert year after year, searching for fresh supplies of food and water. Some of these nomads still live much the way their Stone Age ancestors did. They travel on foot. They search for water-filled melons, roots, and berries. And they skillfully hunt animals for food.

Other nomads are shepherds. They travel great distances across the desert, riding camels or horses. They look for grass and water to feed their large flocks of sheep and goats.

In the Gobi Desert of Asia, where summers are hot and winters are freezing cold, there are nomads that live as traders. For hundreds of years, these people and their camel caravans have traveled the same ancient trails, carrying goods from place to place.

Although different desert people have different customs, different habits, different ways of getting the food and water they need, they all share one thing in common. They know the desert as well as most people know their own neighborhoods. And they particularly know where the desert's life-giving water sources are found.

Where is there water in the desert?

A few desert lands are crossed by rivers. Egypt's Nile flows along a 1,000-mile (1,600-kilometer) stretch of the Sahara. The Colorado River crosses part of the North American Desert.

But most deserts have hidden water sources— underground springs or rivers that flow far below the ground. Now and then, this underground water bubbles up to the surface through a break in the rocks. And wherever it does, an *oasis*—an area of green, growing things—appears.

An oasis can be small, no more than a few trees and shrubs. Or it can be large enough to hold a good-sized city. It all depends on how much water reaches the surface of the ground. But no matter how big or small these oases are, every desert nomad knows *where* they are—and how precious their water can be.

How does the desert help us?

Water is, of course, the desert's life-giving gift. But there are many other valuable things to be found in the world's deserts.

Precious metals like gold and silver have been dug out of the North American Desert. Vast amounts of oil flow beneath the deserts of Asia and Africa. Nitrates —excellent fertilizers—come from the Atacama Desert of South America. Highly prized minerals, such as uranium, salt, copper, diamonds, borax, gypsum, and phosphates, are found in many of the world's deserts.

Perhaps the most valuable desert resource of all is the land itself. The world's deserts are a kind of land bank. With the right knowledge and skills, they can be made into rich farmland.

Some of these skills have already been developed and put into action. The results have been amazing. California's Imperial Valley was once a wasteland of dry desert. Today it is a rich, productive farming area—thanks to a number of dams that control the water flow of the Colorado River, and a series of canals that bring the water to the valley's fields.

Israel has combined modern-day knowledge with a 2,000-year-old system of wells and ditches. As a result, the Negev Desert blooms again today as it did in ancient times.

What will the future bring?

Land is far too valuable to be misused. In the past, overgrazing or overplanting destroyed usable land and turned it into desert wasteland. Today, some of the world's deserts have already been made productive again. In the future, we may reclaim even more of these harsh, yet strangely beautiful lands we call deserts.